Shall We Know One Another in Heaven

Shall We Know One Another in Heaven

J.C. RYLE
with
C.H. SPURGEON
D.L. MOODY
BILLY SUNDAY
R. MURRAY M'CHEYNE

AMBASSADOR
Belfast • Greenville

Shall We Know One Another in Heaven

ISBN 1 898787 82 4

AMBASSADOR PRODUCTIONS LTD
Providence House
16 Hillview Avenue
Belfast BT5 6JR, UK.

Emerald House Group, Inc.
1 Chick Springs Road, Suite 102
Greenville, South Carolina 29606, USA

Contents

Foreword 7

Who Will Be In Heaven? 9

A Voice From Heaven 23

Shall We Know One Another In Heaven? 45

Heaven Is A Place 57

Blessed Are The Dead 71

Foreword

Heaven! What a breathtaking subject. For the child of God it is our eternal hope. It is the exhilarating prospect that awaits the redeemed of the Lord at the end of the journey. As we, inevitably, approach the eventide of life we consciously realise the best is yet to be. Then, Heaven, the subject of our present reflection and meditation, will have become a sweet reality.

You see, dear friend, Heaven is a wonderful place! Why? Because it is full of wonders. It is something that will never cease to surprise us. It will transcend our wildest dreams. It will outshine even our highest thoughts and fondest musings. It will gloriously surpass our treasured notions and preconceived theories. These and so much more will fade into oblivion and pale gently into insignificance in the unshaded light of His untarnished Throne.

Both Paul and John were spoiled for life on planet earth after they had walked in wonderland. They were never the same again! It was an unexpected trip - but one the erstwhile duo would never forget. The impressions were indelible. They could hardly wait to get back - permanently! They had a preview of glory as the curtain was drawn aside. Their appetites had been whetted to such an extent that they channelled their energies into sharing with others the discoveries they made on their memorable mission.

That is precisely the reason why we have compiled this excellent ministry from five noble worthies of a past generation. They're all different! They have made their mark for God. In their anointed preaching they have left us a rich and valuable heritage. Even with the passing of years the message is untainted by time. It is fresh and fragrant. It is witty and wholesome. It is serious and sublime. It is punchy and spot-on target.

When reading their priceless legacy I felt as though I was standing on the verge of Heaven itself. It became nearer and dearer. Earth seemed to recede as the horizons of that better land came within the grasp of faith. All else seemed as nothing in comparison to the sheer ecstacy and pure delight of beholding the King in all His beauty.

Oh, to be there, with our friends and loved ones! That is the unspeakable thrill of present anticipation amid scenes of rising expectancy. Somehow I sense it will not be very much longer! But, to be there with Jesus, our wonderful Saviour, eternally, that will be Glory, yes. Glory for me!

Reading through these pages your heart will be warmed with the realisation that there are exciting days ahead. Yes, we are born for Glory, we're bound for Glory. We're going home! Perhaps, we need to pray, before going any further, that God would make us homesick for Heaven.

Samuel Gordon,
Loughborough, August 1989

Who Will Be In Heaven?

D. L. MOODY
1837-1899

*'Eternity to the godly is a day
that has no sunset
Eternity to the wicked is a night
that has no sunrise.'*

THOMAS WATSON

1

Who Will Be In Heaven?

D. L. MOODY

*"Let not your heat be troubled: ye believe in God, believe
also in me. In my Father's house are many mansions: if it
were not so, I would have told you. I go to prepare a
place for you. And if I go and prepare a place for you, I
will come again, and receive you unto myself; that where
I am, there ye may be also."*
- John 14:1-3.

I was on my way to a meeting one night with a friend; and he
asked, as we were drawing near the church, "Mr. Moody,
what are you going to preach about?"

"I am going to preach about Heaven," I said, I noticed a
scowl passing over his face, and I said, "What makes you
look so?"

"Why, your subject of Heaven. What's the use of talking
upon a subject that's all speculation? It's only wasting time
on a subject about which you can only speculate."

My answer to that friend was, "If the Lord doesn't want us
to speak about Heaven, He would never have told us about

such a place in the Scriptures; and as Timothy says, 'All scripture is given by inspiration of God, and is profitable...'"

There's no part of the Word of God that is not profitable, and I believe if men would read more carefully these Scriptures they would think more of Heaven. If we want to get men to fix their hearts and attention upon Heaven, we must get them to read more about it.

Men who say that Heaven is a speculation have not read their Bibles. In the blessed Bible there are allusions scattered all through it. If I were to read to you all the passages about Heaven from Genesis to Revelation, it would take me all night and tomorrow to do it. When I took some of the passages lately and showed them to a lady, "Why," said she, "I didn't think there was so much about Heaven in the Bible."

If I were to go into a foreign land and spend my days there, I would like to know all about it; I would like to read all about it. I would want to know all about its climate, its inhabitants, customs, privileges, its government. I would find nothing about that land that would not interest me.

Heaven Is To Be Our Long Home: We Should Learn All We Can About It

Suppose you all were going away to Africa, to Germany, to China, and were going to make one of those places your home, and suppose that I had just come from one of those countries. How eagerly you would listen to what I had to say. I can imagine how the old, grey-haired men and the young men and the deaf would crowd around and put up their hands to learn something about it.

But there is a country in which you are to spend your whole future and you are listless about what kind of country it is. My friends, where are you going to spend eternity? Your life here is very brief. Life is but an inch of time; it is but a span, but a fibre, which will soon be snapped, and you will be ushered into eternity. Where are you going to spend it? If I were to ask you who are going to spend eternity in Heaven

12

to stand up, nearly every one of you would rise. There is not a man here, not one in Chicago, who has not some hope of reaching Heaven. Now, if we are going to spend our future there, it becomes us to go to work and find out all about it.

Heaven Is A Real Place

I call your attention to this truth that Heaven is just as much a place as Chicago. It is a destination; it is a locality. Some people say there is no Heaven. Some men will tell you this earth is all the heaven we have. Queer kind of heaven this. Look at the poverty, the disease in the city! Look at the men out of employment walking around our streets, and then say this is Heaven? How low a man has gotten when he comes to think this way! There is a land where the weary are at rest; there is a land where there is peace and joy, where no sorrow dwells, and as we think of it and speak about it, how sweet it looms up before us.

I remember soon after I got converted, a pantheist got hold of me and tried to draw me back to the world. Those men who try to get hold of a young convert are the worst set of men. I don't know a worse man than he who tries to pull young Christians down. He is nearer the borders of hell than any man I know. When this man knew I had found Jesus he just tried to pull me down. He tried to argue with me. I did not know the Bible very well then, and he got the best of me. The only way to get the best of those atheists, pantheists, or infidels is to have a good knowledge of the Bible. Well, this pantheist told me God was everywhere - in the air, in the sun, in the moon, in the earth, in the stars - but really he meant nowhere. The next time I went to pray it seemed as if I were not praying anywhere or to anyone.

Heaven Is Not Far Away

We have ample evidence in the Bible that there is such a place as Heaven, and we have abundant manifestation that His influence from Heaven is felt among us. He is not in

13

person among us, only in Spirit. The sun is about 95,000,000 miles from the earth, yet we feel its rays. In II Chronicles we read, "If my people, which are called by my name, shall humble themselves, and pray, and seek my face, and turn from their wicked ways; then I will hear from heaven, and will forgive their sin, and heal their land." Here is one reference, and when it is read, a great many people might ask, "How far is Heaven away? can you tell us that?" I don't know how far it is away, but there is one thing I can tell you. He can hear prayer as soon as the words are uttered. There has not been a prayer said that He has not heard; not a tear shed that He has not seen. We don't want to learn the distance. What we want to know is that God is there, and Scripture tells us that.

Turn to I Kings 8:30 and we read, "And hearken thou to the supplication of thy servant, and of thy people Israel, when they shall pray toward this place: and hear thou in heaven thy dwelling place: and when thou hearest, forgive." Now, it is clearly taught in the Word of God that the Father dwells there. It is His dwelling place; and in Acts 7:55 we see that Jesus is there, too. "But he, being full of the Holy Ghost, looked up steadfastly into heaven, and saw the glory of God, and Jesus standing on the right hand of God." And by the eye of faith we can see Him there tonight, too. By faith we shall be brought into His presence, and we shall be satisfied when we gaze upon Him.

Stephen, when he was surrounded by the howling multitude, saw the Son of Man there. When Jesus looked down upon earth and saw this first martyr in the midst of his persecutors, He looked down and gave him welcome. We'll see Him by and by.

It is not the jasper streets and the golden gates that attract us to Heaven. What are your golden palaces on earth; what is it that makes them so sweet? It is the presence of some loving wife or fond children. Let them be taken away and the charm of your home is gone. And so it is Christ who is the

14

charm of Heaven to the Christian. Yes, we shall see Him there. How sweet the thought that we shall dwell with Him forever, and shall see the nails in His hands and in His feet which He received for us.

Jesus And Loved Ones Make Heaven Sweet

I read a little story not long since which went to my heart. A mother was on the point of death and the child was taken away from her in case it would annoy her. It was crying continually to be taken to its mother, and teased the neighbours. By and by the mother died and the neighbours thought it was better to bury the mother without letting the child see her dead face. They thought the sight of the dead mother would not do the child any good so they kept it away.

When the mother was buried and the child was taken back to the house, the first thing she did was to run into her mother's sitting room and look all around it, and from there to the bedroom; but no mother was there. She went all over the house crying, "Mother, Mother!" but the child could not find her, and coming to the neighbour, said, "Take me back, I don't want to stay here if I cannot see my mother." It wasn't the home that made it so sweet to the child. It was the presence of the mother. And so it is not Heaven that is alone attractive to us; it is the knowledge that Jesus, our Leader, our Brother, our Lord, is there.

And the spirits of loved ones whose bodies we have laid in the earth will be there. We shall be in good company there. When we reach that land we shall meet all the Christians who have gone before us. We are told in Matthew, too, that we shall meet angels there, "Take heed that ye despise not one of these little ones; for I say unto you, That in heaven their angels do always behold the face of my Father which is in heaven." Yes, the angels are there and we shall see them when we get Home.

He is there, and where He is, His disciples shall be, for He has said, "I go to prepare a place for you... that where I am, there ye may be also." I believe that when we die the spirit leaves the body and goes to the mansion above, and by and by the body will be resurrected and it shall see Jesus.

Very often people come to me and say, "Mr. Moody, do you think we shall know each other in Heaven?" Very often it is a mother who has lost a dear child and who wishes to see it again. Sometimes it is a child who has lost a mother, a father, and who wants to recognise them in Heaven.

There is just one verse in Scripture in answer to this, and that is, "We shall be satisfied." It is all I want to know. My brother who went up there the other day, I shall see, because I will be satisfied. We will see all those we loved on earth up there, and if we loved them here, we will love them ten thousand times more when we meet them there.

The Greatest Cause Of Rejoicing

Another thought. In chapter 10 of Luke we are told our names are written there if we are Christians. Christ just called His disciples up and paired them off and sent them out to preach the Gospel. Two of us - Mr. Sankey and myself - going about preaching the Gospel, is nothing new. You will find them away back eighteen hundred years ago going off two by two, like Brothers Bliss and Whittle, and Brothers Needham and Stebbins, to different towns and villages. They had gone out, and there had been great revivals in all the cities, towns and villages they had entered. Everywhere they had met with the greatest success. Even the very devils were subject to them. Disease had fled before them. When the disciples met a lame man they said to him, "You don't want to be lame any longer,' and he walked. When they met a blind man they but told him to open his eyes, and behold, he could see.

They came to Christ and rejoiced over their great success, and He said to them, "Notwithstanding in this rejoice not, that the spirits are subject unto you; but rather rejoice, because your names are written in heaven." How are you going to rejoice if your names are not written there?

While I was speaking about this some time ago, a man told me we were preaching a very ridiculous doctrine when we preached this doctrine of assurance. I ask you in all candour, what are you going to do with this assurance if we don't preach it? It is stated that our names are written there; blotted out of the book of death and transferred to the Book of Life.

While in Europe I was travelling with a friend - she is in this hall tonight. On one occasion, we were journeying from London to Liverpool, and the question was put as to where we would stop. We said we would go to the Northwestern, at Lime Street, as that was the hotel where Americans generally stopped. When we got there the house was full; could not let us in. Every room was engaged. But this friend said, "I am going to stay here; I engaged a room ahead. I sent a telegram on."

Sending Their Names In Ahead

My friends, that is just what the Christians are doing - sending their names in ahead. They are sending a message up saying, "Lord Jesus, I want one of those mansions You are preparing; I want to be there." That is what they're doing. And every man and woman here who wants one, if you have not already gotten one, had better make up your mind. Send you names up now.

I would rather a thousand times have my name written in the Lamb's Book than have all the wealth of the world rolling at my feet. A man may get station in this world - but it will prove a bauble - "What shall it profit a man if he shall gain the whole world and lose his own soul?" It is a solemn question. Let it go around the hall tonight - "Is my name written in the Book of Life?"

I can imagine that man down there saying, "Yes; I belong to the Presbyterian church; my name is on the church's

17

books." It may be, but God keeps His books in a different fashion than that in which the church records of this city are kept. You may belong to a good many churches; you may be an elder or a deacon, and be a bright light in your church, yet you may not have your name written in the Book of Life.

Judas was one of the twelve, yet he didn't have his name written in the Book of Life. Satan was among the elect - he dwelt among the angels, yet he was cast from the high hallelujahs.

Is your name written in the Book of life?

A man told me, when I was speaking upon this subject, "That is all nonsense you are speaking." A great many men here are of the same opinion; but I would like them to turn to Daniel, chapter 12, verse 1, "... and there shall be a time of trouble, such as never was since there was a nation even to that same time: and at that time thy people shall be delivered, every one that shall be found written in the book." Everyone shall be delivered whose name shall be written in the Book. We find Paul, in the letters which he wrote to the Philippians, addressing them as those "...true yokefellow...my fellow labourers, whose names are in the book of life."

Let us not be deceived in this. We see it too plainly throughout the Holy Word. In Revelation 21:27 we have three different passages referring to it and in almost the last words in the Scriptures we read, "And there shall in no wise enter into it any thing that defileth, neither whatsoever worketh abomination, or maketh a lie: but they which are written in the Lamb's book of life."

My friends, you will never see that city unless your names are written in that Book of Life. It is a solemn truth. Let it go home to everyone, and sink into the hearts of all here tonight. Don't build your hopes on a false foundation: don't build your hopes on an empty profession. Be sure your name is written there.

Make Sure Your Children Are Ready For Heaven, Too!

The next thing after your own names are written there is to see that the names of the children God has given you are recorded there. Let the fathers and mothers assembled tonight hear this and take it to their hearts. See that your children's names are written there. Ask your conscience if the name of your John, your Willie, your Mary, your Alice is recorded in the Book of Life. If not, make it the business of your life, rather than to pile up wealth for them; make it the one object of your existence to secure for them eternal life, rather than to pave the way to their death and ruin. I read some time ago of a mother in an eastern city who was stricken with consumption. At her dying hour she requested her husband to bring the children to her. The oldest one was brought first and she laid her hand on his head and gave him her blessing and dying message. The next one was brought and she gave him the same. One after another came to her bedside until the little infant was brought in. She took it and pressed it to her bosom, and the people in the room, fearing that she was straining her strength took the child away from her. As this was done she turned to her husband and said, "I charge you, Sir, bring all those children home with you."

And so God charges us. The promise is to ourselves and to our children. We can have our names written there; and then by the grace of God, we can call our children to us and know their names are also recorded there. That great roll is being called, and those bearing the names are summoned every day, every hour; that great roll is being called tonight, and if your name were shouted, could you answer with joy?

You have heard of a soldier who fell in our war. While he lay dying, he was heard to cry, "Here! here." Some of his comrades went up to him thinking he wanted water, but he said, "They are calling the roll of Heaven and I am answer-

19

ing," and in a faint voice he whispered, "Here!" and passed away to Heaven.

If that roll were called tonight, would you be ready to answer, "Here!"? I am afraid not. Let us wake up; may every child of God wake up tonight. There is work to do. Fathers and mothers, look to your children. If I could only speak to one class, I would preach to parents and try to show them the great responsibility that rests upon them - try to teach them how much more they should devote their lives to secure the immortal treasure of Heaven for their children, than to spend their lives in scraping together worldly goods for them.

Pray For Me, Father?

There is a man living on the Mississippi River. The world calls him rich, but if he could bring back his first born son he would give up all his wealth. The boy was brought home one day unconscious. When the doctor examined him he turned to the father, who stood at the bedside, and said, "There is no hope."

"What!" exclaimed the father, "is it possible my boy has to die?"

"There is no hope," replied the doctor.

"Will he not come to?" asked the father.

"He may resume consciousness, but he cannot live," said the doctor.

"Try all your skill, Doctor; I don't want my boy to die," replied the father.

By and by the boy regained a glimmering of consciousness and when he was told that his death was approaching, he said to his father, "Won't you pray for my lost soul, Father? You have never prayed for me." The old man only wept. It was true. During the seventeen years that God had given him his boy he had never spent an hour in prayer for his soul. The object of his life had been to accumulate wealth for that first born son. Am I speaking to a prayerless father or mother tonight? Settle the question of your soul's salvation and pray for the son or the daughter God has given you.

Another Incident

But I have another anecdote to tell. It was Ralph Wells who told me of this one. A certain gentleman had been a member of the Presbyterian Church. His little boy was sick. When he went home his wife was weeping and she said, "Our boy is dying. He has had a change for the worse. I wish you would go in and see him." The father went into the room and placed his hand on the brow of his dying boy and could feel that the cold, damp sweat was gathering there; that the cold, icy hand of Death was feeling for the chords of life.

"Do you know, my boy, that you are dying?" asked the father.

"Am I? Is this death? Do you really think I am dying?" questioned the boy.

"Yes, my son, your end on earth is near," replied the father.

"And will I be with Jesus tonight, Father?" asked the boy.

"Yes, you will be with the Saviour." comforted the father.

"Father, don't you weep, for when I get there I will go right straight to Jesus and tell Him you have been trying all my life to lead me to Him," said the boy.

God has given me two little children, and ever since I can remember I have directed them to Christ. I would rather they carried this message to Jesus - that I had tried all my life to lead them to Him - than have all the crowns of the earth; would rather lead them to Jesus than give them the wealth of the world.

Mothers and fathers, the little ones may begin early; be in earnest with them now. You know not how soon you may be taken from them , or they may be taken from you. Therefore let this impression be made upon their minds that you care for their souls a million times more than for their worldly prospects. And if you yourself have never thought how little it would profit you to gain the whole world and lose your own soul, I beseech you not to let another sun go down before you are able to say that *your* name has been written in heaven.

A Voice From Heaven

C. H. SPURGEON
1834-1892

*'Faint not - the miles to Heaven
are few and short!'*

SAMUEL RUTHERFORD

2

A Voice From Heaven

C.H. SPURGEON

"And they heard a great voice from heaven, saying unto them, Come up hither."
- Revelation 11:12.

Waiving all attempts at explaining the text from its connection, I intend to use it as the voice of God to His people.

I. A SUMMONS SENT TO EVERY SAINT

We shall regard it, first of all, as a summons sent at the appointed hour to every saint. When the time shall come, fixed by irreversible decree, there shall be heard 'a great voice from heaven' to every believer in Christ, saying, "Come up hither."

1. A Joyful Anticipation

This should be to each one of us who be in Christ the subject of very joyful anticipation. Instead of dreading the time when we shall leave this world to go to the Father, we should be thirsting and panting for the hour that shall set our

25

soul at liberty and give our spirit once for all its full discharge from an imprisonment of clay and from the bondage of "the body of this death."

To some Christians it will be not only joyful in anticipation but intensely delightful when it arrives. It is not true, as some suppose, that when death really appears it is necessarily a dreadful and hideous apparition.

> **Death no terrific foe appears;**
> **An angel's lovely form he wears;**
> **A friendly messenger he proves**
> **To every soul whom Jesus loves.**

I doubt not that many believers welcome the kind of approach of death as the arrival of their best friend and salute their last hour with intense delight.

Witness the saint who has been for years bed-ridden. She is tossed to and fro as on a sea of pains, never resting at the anchorage of ease. She cries at night, *Would God 'twere morning!* And when the light of day affects her eyes, she longs for the returning darkness that she may slumber for a little season and forget her pains. her bones have worn through her skin by long lying upon a bed made as soft as kindness can render it but still too hard for so weak and tormented a body. Pangs have shot through her frame as arrows piercing the foe. Every vein has been a river flushed with agony, every nerve a telegraph conveying messages of pain to the spirit.

Oh, how welcome shall it be when the voice shall cry from Heaven, "Come up hither!" No more weakness now! The joyful spirit shall leave all bodily pain behind. The last tear shall be wiped away by the Divine Father's hand, and she who was a mass of disease and decay shall now become an embodiment of intense delight, full to the brim with satisfaction and infinite pleasure. In that land where Jehovah-Rophi reigns, the inhabitants shall no more say, "I am sick."

With what joy will the voice from Heaven sound in the ear of the man wearied with labour! The world shall know of some of us when we die that we have not been idle but have served our God beyond our strength. He who finds the ministry an easy profession shall find the flames of Hell no pleasant resting-place.

There may be some of you in whose name I can speak now who have served God with throbbing brow and with palpitating heart. You are weary in your Master's service but never weary of it - springing to the collar when the load was far too heavy for your single strength. You are ready to labour or ready for fight, never putting off your armour but standing harnessed both by night and day, crying in your Master's name,

> Is there a foe before whose face
> I fear His cause to plead?
> Is there a lamb among His flock
> I would refuse to feed?

The time must come when age shall take away the juvenile vigour which for a while carried off weariness, and you shall be constrained to lament, "When shall the shadows be drawn out? When shall I fulfil as a hireling my day?" Happy for the minister, if in his pulpit he shall hear the voice, "Come up hither,' and shall

> His body and his charge lay down,
> And cease at once to work and live.

Happy for you, fellow-labourers in the kingdom of Christ and in the tribulation of our common Saviour, if just when you think you can do no more, your doing shall be ended and your reward shall come and your Saviour shall say, "Come up hither," and you shall see the glory which you have believed in upon earth.

Beloved, with what intense delight will death be hailed by the sons of abject poverty; I mean "such as are of the household of faith." From shivering in the winter's cold to the brightness of Heaven; from the solitude and desolation of friendless penury to the communion and fellowship of saints made perfect; from the poor emaciated bones; from the form ready to be bowed down with hunger; from the tongue that cleaveth to the mouth with thirst; from crying children and a wailing wife - wailing for bread, crying that they may be fed - oh, to be snatched away to Heaven!

Happy man, to have known so much of ill, that he may know the better the sweetness of perfect bliss! Mansions of the blessed, how bright ye are in contrast with the cotter's hut! Streets of gold, how ye shall make the beggar forget the cold doorstep and dry arch! Paupers become princes; pensioners are peers, and the peasants are kings and priests. O land of Goshen, how long before the sons of Israel receive thee for an heritage!

Dear friends, I think I ought to add to this - with what seraphic joy must this voice have been heard in the martyrs' ears! In caves and dens of the earth where the holy wander in their sheepskins and goatskins, what holy triumph must this message create!

Blandina, tossed in the Roman amphitheatre on the horns of bulls, then seated in her red-hot iron chair and mocked while she is there consumed before the jeering multitude - oh, how that voice, "Come up hither!" must have cheered her in those horrid agonies which she bore with more than masculine heroism.

The many who have perished on the rack - surely they have seen visions like those of Stephen who, when the stones were rattling about his ears, saw Heaven open and heard the Heaven-sent voice, "Come up hither."

The multitude of our ancestors - our venerated predecessors who carried the banner of the cross before our day, who stood on flaming faggots and bore the flames with patience, with their bodies consumed by fire till their lower limbs were burnt away and life just remained within a mass of ashes - oh, the joy with which they would leap into their fiery chariots, drawn by horses of fire straight to Heaven, at this omnipotent bidding of the Master, "Come up hither!"

Though yours and mine may never be the lot of protracted sickness, or abject penury, or excessive labour, or the death or martyrdom, yet let us still believe that if we are true followers of Christ, whenever death shall come, or rather whenever life and immortality shall come, it shall be a joyous and blessed time for us.

Seek not of the Most High to delay the time when He shall summon thee to the upper chamber, but listen every morning, with a heart desiring to hear it; listen for the royal message which saith, "Come up hither."

An ancient singer sweetly words it -

I said sometimes with tears,
Ah me! I'm loth to die!
Lord, silence Thou these fears;
My life's with Thee on high.
Sweet truth to me!
I shall arise,
And with these eyes
My Saviour see.

What means my trembling heart,
To be thus shy of death?
My life and I shan't part,
Though I resign my breath.
Sweet truth to me!
I shall arise,
And with these eyes
My Saviour see.

29

hen welcome harmless grave!
By Thee to Heaven I'll go:
y Lord, Thy death shall save
Me from the flames below.
Sweet truth to me!
I shall arise,
And with these eyes
My Saviour see.

2. We Should Patiently Wait For The Voice From Heaven

While this should be the subject of joyous anticipation, it should also be *the object of patient waiting*. God knows best when it is time for us to be bidden, "Come up hither."

We must not wish to antedate the period of our departure. I know that strong love will make us cry,

O Lord of Hosts the waves divide
And land us all in Heaven;

but patience must have her perfect work.

I would not wish to die while there is more work to do or more souls to win, more jewels to place in the Redeemer's crown, more glory to be given to His name, and more service to be rendered to His church.

When George Whitefield lay sick and wanted to die, his black nurse who had prayed for him said, "No Massa Whitefield, there is no dying for you. Many a poor Negro is yet to be brought to Christ, and you must live." And live he did.

When Melancthon lay very sick, Martin Luther said he should not die. And when his prayers began to work a cure, Melancthon said, "Let me die, Luther, let me die. Leave off your prayers." But Luther said, "No, man, I want you, God's cause wants you, and you shall not die yet." Then when Melancthon refused to eat or take the necessary medicine because he hoped to be soon with Christ, Luther threatened him with excommunication if he did not there and then do as he was bidden.

It is not for us by neglect of means, or wanton waste of strength or profligate zeal, to cut short a life which may be useful. "Do thyself no harm" - the advice of the jailor to Paul - is not at all amiss here.

God knows the pace at which time should travel and how long the road of life should be. If it were possible for there to be regrets in Heaven, it might be that we did not live longer here to do more good. More sheaves, more jewels! But how, unless there be more work? True there is the other side of it - that living so briefly we sinned the less and our temptations were the fewer; but when we are fully serving God and He is giving us to scatter precious seed and reap a hundredfold, we would even say it is well for us to abide where we are.

An aged Christian, being asked whether she would rather die or live, said she would rather it should be as God willed it. "But if you might have your choice, which would you have?" She said, "I would ask God to choose for me, for I should be afraid to choose for myself."

So be you ready to stay on this side of Jordan or to cross the flood, just as your Master wills it.

3. All Should Make Sure Of Salvation Now

As this "Come up hither" should excite joyous anticipation, tempered by patient waiting, so, beloved, it should always be to us *a matter of absolute certainty as to its ultimate reception.*

I would not give sleep to my eyes nor slumber to my eyelids if this were a subject of doubt personally as to whether at the last I should stand among the justified. I can understand a man being in doubt about his interest in Christ, but I cannot understand a man's resting content to be in these doubts. This is a matter about which we want absolute certainty.

Young man yonder, are you sure that the King will say to you, "Come up hither"? If thou believest in the Lord Jesus Christ with all thy heart, that call from the divine throne is as certain to meet thine ear as that other cry, of "Dust thou art, and unto dust thou shalt return." He that believeth on the Son of God hath everlasting life.

No "ifs" or "peradventures" ought to be tolerated in our hearts. I know they will come up like ill weeds; but it is ours to pull them, heap them together and set them on fire, as farmers do with the twitch in their furrows. The Devil loves for us to cast lots at the foot of the cross, but Christ would have us look unto Him and find a sure salvation.

We are not to be put off with guesswork here. My friend, can you be easy without infallible certainty? You may die tonight and be lost forever!

Man, I charge thee by the living God, shut not those eyes until thou art sure that thou shalt open them either on earth or in Heaven! But if there be this fear that thou mayest lift up those eyes in Hell, how darest thou sleep, lest thy bed become thy tomb and thy chamber become the door of Tophet to thee!

Brethren in Christ, let us seek to have the seal of God upon us, the infallible witness of the Holy Spirit bearing witness with our spirits that we are born of God, so we may both joyfully hope and quietly wait to see the salvation of God when the Master saith, "Come up hither."

4. With Joy Let Us Think About God's Call To Heaven

I think very often, besides joyfully anticipating, patiently waiting and being confidently assured of it, the Christian should *delightfully contemplate it.* Let every Christian now say, "I shall soon be dying: time swiftly speeds away."

I can paint the picture now. They have told me that I am very sick, but they have kept back from me till I asked them plainly the news that I must very speedily die. But now I know it and feel the sentence of death myself.

Now for the joyous secret. In a few minutes I shall know more of Heaven than an assembly of divines could teach me. But how solemn is the scene around me! They are moving quietly about the room. Very silently they are catching each word uttered - treasuring it up.

Now saint, thou must play the man. Say a good word for the Master! Stir the deeps of Jordan with thy bold march of victory, O soldier of Jesus! Make its shelving shores resound with thy melodies now! Show them how a Christian can die. Now let thy full heart overflow with floodtides of glory. Drink thou up the bitter cup and say, "Death is swallowed up in victory."

But, how is this that my mind seems fluttering as though about to take wing -

> What is this absorbs me quite-
> Steals my sense - shuts my sight -
> Drowns my spirit - draws my breath?
> Tell me, my soul, can this be death?

I cannot see; the film is forming on my eyes; the dew from the damps of death. The kind hand of affection has just wiped my forehead. I fain would speak, but there is a throttle in my throat which keeps down the word. This is the monitor to me of the silence of the tomb. I will strive against it.

> Joyful, with all the strength I have,
> My quivering lips shall sing,
> Where is they victory, boasting grave?
> And where's the monster's sting?

The effort has exhausted the dying one. He must fall back again. They stay him up with pillows. Ah, ye may prop him up with pillows, but he has a better arm beneath him than that of the fondest friend. Now doth His beloved "stay him with apples, and comfort him with flagons," for while sick to death, he is also "sick of loves." His Master makes his bed in his sickness. His left hand is under his head, and His right hand doth embrace him. The Husband of that chosen soul is now answering the prayer for his presence which it delighted to offer, saying, "Abide with me" Now is the poet's prayer granted to the letter -

Hold then thy cross before my closing eyes!
Shine through the gloom and point me to the skies!
Heaven's morning breaks and earth's vain shadows
flee;
In life and death, O Lord, abide with me!

We cannot paint the last moment - the rapture, the dawning glory, the first young flash of the beatific glory - we must leave that all. On earth the scene is far more sombre, yet not sad. See you yon friends gather round. They say, "Yes, he is gone. How placidly he slept! I could not tell the moment when he passed from sleep to death. He is gone."

They weep, but not with hopeless sorrow, for they mourn the body, not the soul. The setting is broken, but the gem is safe. The fold is removed, but the sheep is feeding on the hill-tops of Glory. Worms devour the clay, but angels welcome the soul.

There is general mourning wherever the good man was known; but mark ye, it is only in the dark that this sorrow reigns. Up there in the light, what are they doing? That spirit as it left the body found not itself alone. Angels had come to meet it. Angelic spirits clasped the disembodied spirit in their arms and bore it upward beyond the stars - beyond where the angel in the sun keeps his everlasting watch -

beyond, beyond this lower sky immeasurable leagues.

Lo, the pearly gates appear and the azure light of the city of bejewelled walls! The spirit asketh, "Is yonder city the fair Jerusalem where they need no candle, neither light of the sun?" He shall see for himself ere long, for they are nearing the Holy City; and it is time for the cherub-bearers to begin their chorale. The music breaks from the lips of those that convey the saint to Heaven - "Lift up your heads, O ye gates, and be ye lifted up ye everlasting doors, that the blood-bought of the King of glory may come in!" The gates of pearl give way and the joyous crowds of Heaven welcome their brother to the seats of immortality.

But what next, I cannot tell. In vain the fancy strives to paint it. Jesus is there, and the spirit is in His arms. In Heaven, where should it be but in the arms of Jesus? Oh, boundless oceans of joy! I shall see Him! These eyes shall see Him and not another.

> Shall see Him wear that very flesh
> On which my guilt was laid;
> His love intense, His merit fresh,
> As though but newly slain.

> These eyes shall see Him in that day
> The Man who died for me!
> And all my rising bones shall say,
> "Lord, who is like to Thee!"

I could lose myself while talking upon this subject, for my heart is on fire. I wander, but I cannot help it. My heart is far away upon the hills with my beloved Lord. What will the bliss of Glory be? A surprise, I think, even to those who shall obtain it. We shall scarcely know ourselves when we get to Heaven, so surprised we shall be at the difference.

That poor man yonder is to be robed in all the splendours of a king. Come with me and see those bright ones: that son

35

of toil who rests forever; that child of sin, washed by Jesus and now a companion of the God of heaven; and I, the chief of sinners singing out His praise; Saul of Tarsus hymning the music of Calvary; the penitent thief, with his deep bass note, exalting dying love; Magdalene mounting to the alto notes, for there must be some voices even in Heaven which must sing alone and mount to higher notes where the rest of us cannot reach - the whole together singing, "Unto Him that loved us, and hath washed us from our sins in His own blood, unto Him be glory forever and ever."

Oh, that we were there! Oh, that we were there! But we must patiently wait the Master's will. It shall not be long ere He shall say, "Come up hither."

II. GOD'S VOICE, A WHISPER IN THE BELIEVER'S HEART

Now to a second part of the subject. We will take the test this time, not as a summons to depart but as a whisper from the skies to the believer's heart. There is a voice that sounds from Heaven tonight, not as a peremptory summons but as a gently-whispered invitation - "Come up hither."

The Father seems to say this to every adopted child. We say, "Our Father which art in heaven." The Father's heart desires to have His children round His knee; and His love each day beckons us with a tender "Come up hither." Nor will your Father and my Father ever be content till every one of His children are in the many mansions above.

And *Jesus* whispers this in your ear tonight, too. Hearken! Do you not hear Him say, "I will that they also whom thou hast given to me be with me where I am, that they may behold my glory - the glory which thou hast given me - the glory which I had with thee before the world was?" Jesus beckons thee to the skies, believer. Lay not fast hold upon things of earth. He who is but a lodger in an inn must not live as though he were at home. Keep thy tent ready for striking. Be thou

36

ever prepared to draw up thine anchor and to sail across the sea to the better port, for while Jesus beckons, here we have no continuing city.

No true wife hath rest save in the house of her husband. Where her consort is, there is her home - a home which draws her soul towards it every day. Jesus, I say, invites us to the skies. He cannot be completely content until He brings His body, the church, into the glory of its Head and conducts His elect spouse to the marriage feast of her Lord.

Besides the desires of the Father and the Son, all those who have gone before seem to be leaning over the battlements of Heaven and calling, "Courage, brothers! Courage, brothers! Eternal glory awaits you. Fight your way, stem the current, breast the wave, and come up hither. Without you we cannot be made perfect; there is no perfect church in Heaven till all the chosen saints be there; therefore come up hither." They stretch out their hands of fellowship; they look with glistening eyes of strong affection upon us; still again they say, "Come up hither."

Warriors who wear your laurels, ye call us to the brow of the hill where the like triumphs await us. The angels do the same tonight. How they must wonder to see us so careless, so worldly, so hardened! They also beckon us away and cry from their starry seats, "Beloved, ye over whom we rejoiced when you were brought as prodigals to your Father's house, come up hither, for we long to see you. Your story of grace will be a strange and wondrous one - one which angels love to hear."

> Stretch your wings, ye saints, and fly,
> Straight to yonder worlds of joy.

I have kept my pledge to be short on that point. You can walk in this meditation as in a garden when you are quiet and alone. All nature rings the bell which calls you to the Temple above. You may see the stars at night looking down like the eyes of God upon you and saying, "Come up hither." The whispers of the wind as they come in the stillness of the night talk to you and say, "There is another and better land; come away with us; come up hither." Yes, every cloud that sails across the sky may say to you, "Mount up beyond me into the clear ether which no cloud can dim, and behold the sun which I can never hide - the noon which I can never mar. Come up hither."

III. A VOICE FROM HEAVEN CALLS EVERY UNCONVERTED PERSON

I shall want your attention to my third point for a few minutes, for I think these words may be used as a loving invitation to the unconverted. There are many spirit voices which cry to them, "Come up hither; come up to Heaven."

I like to see so many crowding here on these dark, cold, wintry days. This huge place is just as crowded as though it were some little vestry. you press upon one another as did the throngs in the days of the Master. God gives a spirit of hearing nowadays in a most wonderful manner. And I would that while you are hearing, some living spark of divine fire may fall into your hearts and become the parent of a glowing fire.

If we ask any man whether he desires to go to Heaven, he will say, "Yes"; but his desires for Heaven are not strong enough to be of practical use. They are such sorry winds, that there is no sailing to heaven with them. Perhaps if we can quicken those desires tonight, God the Spirit may bless our words to the bringing of men into the way of life.

Sinner, wanderer far from God, many voices salute thee. Albeit thou hast chosen the paths of the destroyer, there are many who would turn thee to the way of peace.

1. First, God Our Father Calls Thee

Thou asketh, "How?" Sinner, thou hast had many troubles of late. Business goes amiss. Thou has been out of work. Thou has tried to get on, but thou canst not do it. In thy house everything is out of order. you are always floundering from one slough into another; ye are growing weary of your life.

Dost thou not know, sinner, this is thy Father saying, "Come up hither"? Thy portion is not here; seek thou another and a better land. Thou has built thy nest on a tree that is marked for the axe and he is pulling thy nest down for thee that thou mayest build on the rock. I tell you, these troubles are but love-strokes to deliver thee from thyself.

If thou hadst been left unchastised, I had had little hope of thee. Surely then, God would have said, "Let him alone; he will have no portion in the next life; let him have his portion here."

We heard of a godly wife who for twenty years had been persecuted by a brutal husband - a husband so excessively bad that her faith at last failed her. She ceased to be able to believe that he would ever be converted. But all the while she was more kind to him than ever.

One night at twelve o'clock, in a drunken debauch he told his friends he had such a wife as no other man had, and if they would go home with him, he would knock her up, but she should get supper for them.

They came, and the supper was very soon ready, consisting of such things as she had prepared as well and as rapidly as the occasion would allow. She waited on the table with as much cheerfulness as if the feast had been held at the proper time. She did not utter a word of complaint.

At last, one of the company more sober than the rest asked how it was she could always be so kind to such a husband. Seeing that her conduct had made some little impression, she ventured to say to him, "I have done all I can to bring my husband to God, but I fear he will never be saved. Therefore, his portion must be in Hell for ever so I will make him as happy as I can while he is here, for he has nothing to expect hereafter."

Such is your case tonight. You may get some pleasure here, but you have nothing to expect hereafter. God has been pleased to take your pleasures away. Here, then, I have good hopes that, since He shakes you from the present, you may be driven to the future.

God your Father is making you uncomfortable in order that you may seek Him. It is the beckoning of His love-finger, "Come up hither." Those deaths you have had lately - all say, "Come up hither."

When your mother died - a saint indeed - do you remember what she said to you? "I could die happy if it were not for you and your brother. Oh, that I might have a hope that you may yet come to God."

Do you remember, man, how that little daughter of yours had been to Sunday school. She died so young! She kissed you and said, "Dear father, do give up the drunkard's cup and follow me to Heaven. Father I am dying. Do not be angry because I said that. Father, follow me to Heaven." You have not yielded to that loving entreaty, so you are descending into Hell. All this was God beckoning to you and saying, "Come up hither." He has called and you have refused. Take care lest when you call, He should refuse you.

Besides, you have had a sickness yourself. It is not so long ago since you had a fever, or was it an accident? Everybody said you had a near escape for life. You had time for reflection when you lay in that hospital ward or in your own little room. Do you remember what Conscience said to you? How it rent away the curtain and made you look at your destiny, until you read in fiery letters these words, "Thou shalt make thy bed in Hell."

Oh, how you trembled then! You had no objection to seeing the minister. You could not laugh then at the Gospel of Christ. You made a great many vows and resolutions, but you have broken them all. You have lied unto the Most High. You have perjured yourself to the God of Israel and mocked at the God of mercy and of justice. Beware, lest He take you away with a stroke, for then a great ransom shall not deliver you. These things, then, have been beckonings of your

Father's hand to you, saying, "Come up hither."

2. The Lord Jesus Christ Has Also Beckoned To You To Come

Thou has heard that He made a way to Heaven. What does a way mean? Is not a road an invitation to a traveller to walk therein?

I have crossed the Alps and have seen the mighty roads which Napoleon made so he might take his cannon into Austria. But how shall we compare the works which men have made through the solid granite and over pathless mountains - mountains that before were pathless - with the road which Christ has made to Heaven through the rocks of justice, over the gulfs of sin, throwing Himself into the gaps, leaping Himself into the chasm to complete the way?

Now the way itself speaks to you. The blood of Christ, which made the way, speaks better things than that of Abel. This it says, "Sinner, believe on Christ and thou art saved."

By every drop of blood which streamed in sweat from Him in the garden; by every drop which poured from His hands and feet; by all the agony which He endured, I do beseech thee, hear the voice which crieth, "Go and sin no more." Trust thy soul with Him and thou art saved.

But, my dear hearer, have patience with me, give me thine ear.

3. The Spirit Of God Strives With Thee And Cries, "Come Up Hither"

The Spirit of God wrote this Book, and wherefore was it written? Hear the words of Scripture; "These are written that ye might believe that Jesus is the Christ the Son of God, and that believing, ye might have life through His name."

Here is the Book full of promises, perfumed with affection and brimming with love. Oh, wherefore wilt thou spurn it and put the voice of mercy from thee! Every time thou seest

41

the Bible, think thou seest on its cover, "Go up to Heaven; seek eternal life."

Then there is the ministry through which the Spirit of God speaks. I have often prayed my Master to give me a Baxter's heart to weep for sinners and a Whitefield's tongue to plead. I have neither; but if I had them, how I would plead with you!

But such as I have I give you. As God's ambassador, I do beseech you, sinner, turn from the error of your ways. "As I live, saith the Lord, I have no pleasure in the death of him that dieth, but would rather that he turn unto me and live."

Why will ye die? Is Hell so pleasant? Is an angry God a trifle? Is sin a thing to be laughed at? Is the right hand of God, when bared in thunder, a thing to be despised? Oh, turn to thee! The Spirit bids thee flee to the refuge.

Moreover, does not thy conscience say the same? Is there not something in thy heart which says, Begin to think about your soul; trust thy soul with Christ? May grace Divine constrain you to listen to the still small voice, that you may be saved!

And last of all,

4. The Spirits Of Your Friends Departed Cry From Heaven To You

That voice I would you could hear saying, "Come up hither." Mother - unconverted woman - you have a babe in Heaven; perhaps not one or two, but a family of babes in Heaven. You are a mother of angels, and those young cherubs cry to you, "Mother, come up hither."But this can never be unless you repent and believe in the Lord Jesus Christ.

Some of you have carried to the tomb the most sainted of relatives. Your hoary-headed father at last went the way of all flesh, and from his celestial seat before the eternal throne he cries, "Come up hither."

A sister, sicklied by consumption, who has long since left

your house for you to mourn her absence, cries, "Come up hither."

I adjure you, ye sons of saints in Glory; I adjure you, daughter of immortal mothers; despise not the voice of those who speak from Heaven to you. Were it possible for them to come here to speak to you, I know the notes of fond affection which would spring from your lips - "There's my mother." "There's my father."

They cannot come, but I am the spokesman for them. If I cannot speak as *they* might, yet remember, if ye be not converted when you hear the Gospel preached, "neither would you be converted if one rose from the dead." They could but tell you the Gospel; I do no less; that Gospel is, "Believe on the Lord Jesus Christ, and thou shalt be saved."

"He that believeth and is baptised shall be saved," says the Evangelist. To believe is to trust Christ; to be baptised is not baby sprinkling - for that there is no warrant but in the inventions of man. To be baptised is to be buried with Christ in baptism after faith; for that which is done without faith, and not done of faith, is contrary to the Lord's command. Baptism is for saints, not for sinners: like the Lord's Supper, it is *in* the church, not *out* of it. Baptism does not save you; you are baptised because you are saved. Baptism is the outward recognition of the great inward change which the Spirit of God has wrought.

Believe, then, in Jesus. Flat on thy face before His cross cast thyself now; then rise and say, "Now will I confess His name, be united with His church and believe that at last, having confessed Him before men, He may confess me before my Father which is in Heaven."

Now I am clear of your blood - remember. I suppose there are seven thousand people here tonight who will be without excuse in the day of judgment. I have warned you as best I can. I have pleaded with you. Sinner, thy blood be on thine own head if thou refuse this great salvation.

43

O God the Holy Ghost, make them willing in the day of Thy power and save them this night for Thy name's sake. Amen.

Shall We Know One Another In Heaven?

J. C. Ryle
1816-1900

'Know each other! Blessed comfort!
When this mortal life is o' er,
We shall know our friends departed,
Kindred spirits gone before;
In our holy thrill of transport
They will be the first to share,
First to bid us kindly welcome:
We shall know each other there.'

FANNY CROSBY

Jesus Christ, we hope to go to Heaven. Surely there is nothing unreasonable in asking men to consider the subject of Heaven.

OUR FUTURE HOME

Now what will Heaven be like? The question, no doubt, is a deep one, but there is nothing presumptuous in looking at it. The man who is about to sail for Australia or New Zealand as a settler, is naturally anxious to know something about his future home, its climate, its employments, its inhabitants, its ways, its customs. All these are subjects of deep interest to him. You are leaving the land of your nativity, you are going to spend the rest of your life in a new hemisphere. It would be strange indeed if you did not desire information about your new abode. Now surely, if we hope to dwell for ever in that "better country, even a heavenly one," we ought to seek all the knowledge we can get about it. Before we go to our eternal home we should try to become acquainted with it.

There are many things about Heaven revealed in Scripture. That all who are found there will be of one mind and of one experience, chosen by the same Father, washed in the same blood of atonement, renewed by the same Spirit; that universal and perfect holiness, love, and knowledge will be the eternal law of the kingdom - all these are ancient things, and I do not mean to dwell on them at the moment. Suffice it to say, that Heaven is the eternal presence of everything that can make a saint happy, and the eternal absence of everything that can cause sorrow. Sickness, and pain, and disease, and death, and poverty, and labour, and money, and care, and ignorance, and misunderstanding, and slander, and lying, and strife, and contention, and quarrels, and envies, and jealousies, and bad tempers, and infidelity, and skepticism, and irreligion, and superstition, and heresy, and schism, and wars, and fightings, and bloodshed, and murders, and law suits - all, all these things shall have no place in Heaven. On earth, in this present time, they may life and flourish. In

Heaven even their footprints shall not be known.

Hear what the inspired apostle St. John says: "There shall in no wise enter into it anything that defileth, neither whatsoever worketh abomination, or maketh a lie; but they which are written in the Lamb's book of life." (Rev. 21:27). "There shall be no night there; and they need no candle, neither light of the sun; for the Lord God giveth them light: and they shall reign for ever and ever" (Rev. 22:5). "They shall hunger no more, neither thirst any more; neither shall the sun light on them, nor any heat. For the Lamb which is in the midst of the throne shall feed them, and shall lead them unto living fountains of waters; and God shall wipe away all tears from their eyes" (Rev. 7:16,17). "There shall be no more death, neither sorrow, nor crying, neither shall there be any more pain; for the former things are passed away" (Rev. 21:4).

Hear what the glorious dreamer, John Bunyan says: "I saw in my dream that these two men, Christian and Hopeful, went in at the gate. And lo! as they entered, they were transfigured, and they had raiment put on that shone like gold. There were also that met them with harps and crowns, and gave them to them; the harps to praise withal, and the crowns in token of honour. Then I heard in my dream that all the bells in the city rang again for joy, and that it was said unto them, 'Enter ye into the joy of your Lord.' I also heard the men themselves sing with a loud voice, saying, 'Blessing, and honour, and glory, and power, be unto him that sitteth upon the throne, and unto the Lamb for ever and ever.'

"Now, just as the gates were opened to let in the men, I looked in after them, and behold the city shone like the sun; the streets also were paved with gold, and in them walked many men with crowns on their heads, palms in their hands, and golden harps to sing praises withal.

"There were also of them that had wings and they answered one another without intermission, saying, 'Holy, holy, holy is the Lord.' And after that they shut up the gates; which, when I had seen, I wished myself among them."

SHALL WE KNOW ONE ANOTHER

But I wish to confine myself now to one single point of deep and momentous interest. That point is the mutual recognition of friends in the next world. I want to examine the question, 'Shall we know one another in Heaven?'

Now what saith the Scripture on this subject? This is the only thing I care to know. I grant freely that there are not many texts in the Bible which touch the subject at all. I admit fully that pious and learned divines are not of one mind with me about the matter in hand. I have listened to may ingenious reasonings and arguments against the view that I maintain. But in theology I dare not call any man master and father. My only aim and desire is to find out what the Bible says, and to take my stand upon its teaching.

Let us hear what David said when his child was dead. "Now he is dead, wherefore should I fast? can I bring him back again? I shall go to him, but he shall not return to me" (2 Sam. 12:23). What can these words mean, but that David hoped to see his child, and meet him again, in another world? This was evidently the hope that cheered him, and made him dry his tears. The separation would not be for ever.

Let us hear what St. Paul said to the Thessalonians. "What is our hope, or joy, or crown of rejoicing? Are not even ye in the presence of our Lord Jesus Christ at His coming?" (I Thess. 2:19). These words must surely mean that the apostle expected to recognise his beloved Thessalonian converts in the day of Christ's second advent. he rejoiced in the thought that he would see them face to fact at the last day; would stand side by side with them before the throne, and would be able to say, "Here am I, and the seals which Thou didst give to my ministry."

Let us hear what the same apostle says, in the same epistle, for the comfort of mourners. "I would not have you to be ignorant, brethren, concerning them which are asleep, that ye sorrow not, even as others which have no hope. For if we believe that Jesus died and rose again, even so them also which sleep in Jesus will God bring with Him" (I Thess. 4:13,14). There would be no point in these words of consolation if they did not imply the mutual recognition of saints. The hope with which he cheers wearied Christians is the hope of meeting their beloved friends again. He does not merely say, "Sorrow not, for they are at rest - they are happy - they are free from pain and trouble - they are better off than they would be here below." No! he goes a step further. He says, "God shall bring them with Christ, when He brings them back to the world. You are not parted for ever. You will meet again."

WE SHALL KNOW ONE ANOTHER

I commend these three passages to the reader's attentive consideration. To my eye, they all seem of point to only one conclusion. They all imply the same great truth, that saints in Heaven shall know one another. They shall have the same body and the same character that they had on earth - a body perfected and transformed like Christ's in this transfiguration, but still the same body - a character perfected and purified from all sin, but still the same character. But in the moment that we who are saved shall meet our several friends in Heaven, we shall at once know them, and they will at once know us.

There is some thing to my mind unspeakably glorious in this prospect: few things so strike me in looking forward to the good things yet to come. Heaven will be no strange place to us when we get there. We shall not be oppressed by the cold, shy, chilly feeling that we know nothing of our companions. We shall feel at home. We shall see all of whom we have read in Scripture, and know them all and mark the peculiar graces of each one. We shall look upon Noah, and remember his witness for God in ungodly times. We shall look on Abraham, and remember his faith; on Isaac, and remember his meekness; on Moses, and remember his

51

patience; on David, and remember all his troubles. We shall sit down with Peter, and James, and John and Paul, and remember all their toil when they laid the foundations of the Church. Blessed and glorious will that knowledge and communion be! If it is pleasant to know one or two saints and to meet them occasionally now, what will it be to know them all, and to dwell with them for ever!

There is something unspeakably comforting, more over, as well as glorious in this prospect. It lights up the valley of the shadow of death. It strips the sick bed and the grave of half their terrors. Our beloved friends who have fallen asleep in Christ are not lost, but only gone before. The children of the same God and partakers of the same graces can never be separated very long. They are sure to come together again when this world has passed away. Our pleasant communion with our kind Christian friends is only broken off for a small moment, and is soon to be eternally resumed. These eyes of our shall once more look upon their faces, and these ears of ours shall once more hear them speak. Blessed and happy indeed will that meeting be! - better a thousand times than the parting! We parted in sorrow, and we shall meet in joy; we parted in stormy weather, and we shall meet in a calm harbour; we parted amidst pain and aches, and groans and infirmities: we shall meet with glorious bodies, able to serve our Lord forever without distraction. And, best of all, we shall meet never to be parted, never to shed one more tear, never to put on mourning, never to say good-bye and farewell again. Oh! it is a blessed thought, that saints will know one another in Heaven!

SO MUCH TO TALK ABOUT!

How much there will be to talk about! What wondrous wisdom will appear in everything that we had to go through in the days of our flesh! We shall remember all the way by which we were led, and say, "Goodness and mercy followed me all the days of my life. In my sicknesses and pains, in my losses and crosses, in my poverty and tribulations, in my bereavements and separation, in every bitter cup I had to drink, in every burden I had to carry, in all these was perfect wisdom." We shall see it at last, if we never saw it before, and we shall all see it together, and all untie in praising Him that "led us by the right way to a city of habitation." Surely next to the thought of seeing Christ in Heaven, there is no more blessed and happy thought than that of seeing one another.

Shall we get to Heaven at all? This, after all, is the grand question which the subject should force on our attention, and which we should resume, like men, to look in the face. What shall it profit you and me to study theories about a future state, if we know not on which side we shall be found at the last day? Let us arouse our sleepy minds to a consideration of this momentous question. Heaven, we must always remember, is not a place where all sorts and kinds of persons will go as a matter of course. The inhabitants of Heaven are not such a discordant, heterogeneous rabble as some men seem to suppose. Heaven, it can not be too often remembered, is a prepared place for a prepared people. The dwellers in Heaven will be all of one heart and one mind, one faith and one character. They will be ready for mutual recognition. But are we ready for it? are we in tune? Shall we ourselves get to Heaven?

Why should we not get to Heaven? Let us set that question also before us, and fairly look it in the face. There sits at the right hand of God One who is able to save to the uttermost all them that come unto God by Him, and One who is as willing to save as He is able. The Lord Jesus Christ has died for us on the cross, and paid our mighty debt with His own blood. He is sitting at God's right hand, to be the Advocate and Friend of all who desire to be saved. He is waiting at this moment to be gracious. Surely, if we do not get to Heaven the fault will be all our own. Let us arise and lay hold on the hand that is held out to us from Heaven. Let us never forget that promise, "If we confess our sins, He is faithful and just to forgive us our sins, and to cleanse us from all unrighteousness" (I John 1:9). The prison doors are set wide open; let us go forth and be free. The lifeboat is alongside; let us embark in it and be safe. The bread of life is before us; let us eat and live. The Physician stands before us; let us hear His voice, believe, and make sure our interest in Heaven.

WE SHOULD MEDITATE ON HEAVEN OFTEN

Have we a good hope of going to Heaven, a hope that is Scriptural, reasonable, and will bear investigation? Then let us not be afraid to meditate often on the subject of "Heaven." and to rejoice in the prospect of good things to come. I know that even a believer's heart will sometimes fail when he thinks of the last enemy and the unseen world. Jordan is a cold river to cross at the very best, and not a few tremble when they think of their own crossing. But let us take comfort in the remembrance of the other side. Think, Christian believer, of seeing your Saviour, and beholding your King in His beauty. Faith will be at last swallowed up in sight and hope in certainty. Think of the many loved ones gone before you, and of the happy meeting between you and them. You are not going to a foreign country; you are going home. You are not going to dwell amongst strangers, but amongst friends. You will find them all safe, all well, all ready to greet you, all prepared to join in one unbroken song of praise. Then let us take comfort and persevere. With such prospects before us, we may well cry, "It is worth while to be a Christian!"

I conclude all with a passage from "Pilgrim's Progress," which well deserves reading. Said Pliable to Christian, "What company shall we have in Heaven?"

Christian replied, "There we shall be with seraphim and

cherubim, creatures that will dazzle your eyes to look upon. There, also, you shall meet with thousands and ten thousands that have gone before us to that place; none of them hurtful, but loving and holy; every one walking in the sight of God, and standing in His presence with acceptance for ever. In a word, there we shall see the elders with their golden crowns; there we shall see holy virgins with their golden harps; there we shall see men that by the world were cut in pieces, burnt in flames, eaten of beasts, drowned in the seas, for the love they bore to the Lord of the place; all well, and clothed with immortality as with a garment.

Then said Christian, "The Lord, the Governor of the country, hath recorded *that* in this book; the substance of which is, if we be truly willing to have it. He will bestow it upon us freely."

Then said Pliable, "Well, my good companion, glad am I to hear of these things. Come on, let us mend our pace."

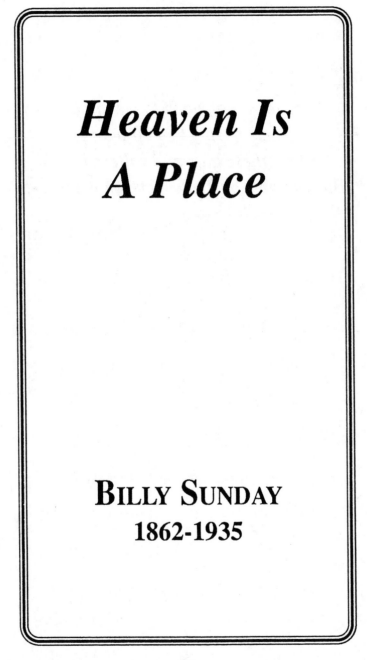

Heaven Is A Place

BILLY SUNDAY
1862-1935

'The scenes of earth to me are dear,
Their beauty I so oft adore;
I love these hills and valleys here,
But thoughts of Heaven charm me more.'

NOEL GRANT

4

Heaven Is A Place

BILLY SUNDAY

*"Let not your heart be troubled: ye believe in God,
believe also in me. In my Father's house are many
mansions: if it were not so, I would have told you. I go to
prepare a place for you. And if I go and prepare a place
for you, I will come again, and receive you unto myself;
that where I am, there ye may be also. And whither I go
ye know, and the way ye know. Thomas saith unto him,
Lord, we know not whither thou goest; and how can we
know the way? Jesus saith unto him, I am the way, the
truth, and the life; no man cometh unto the Father, but by
me." - John 14:1-6.*

Everybody wants to go to Heaven.
We are all curious. We want to know:
Where Heaven is,
How it looks,
Who are there,
What they wear,
And how to get there.

Some say Heaven is a state or a condition. You are wrong. Your home is not a state or a condition; it is a place. The penitentiary is not a state or a condition; it is a place.

Jesus said: "I go to prepare a place for you... that where I am, there ye may be also."

The only source of information we have about Heaven is the Bible. It tells us that God's throne is in the heavens and that the earth is His footstool. And if our spiritual visions are not blinded, we believe it is true.

Enoch walked with God and was not, for God took him to Heaven. He left this earth at the behest of God and went to Heaven where God has His dwelling place.

Elijah, when his mission on earth was finished, in the providence of God, was wafted to Heaven in a chariot of fire. The former pupils went to search for the translated prophet, but they did not find him.

But it was the privilege of Peter, James and John on the Mount of Transfiguration with Jesus to see the gates of Heaven open and two spirits jump down on the earth whom they recognised as Moses and Elijah, who so may years before had walked through Palestine and had warned the people of their sins and had slain 450 of the false prophets of Baal.

When Jesus began His public ministry, we are told the heavens opened and God stopped making worlds and said from Heaven; "This is my beloved Son. Hear ye him."

Then Stephen, with his face lit up with the glories of the Celestial Kingdom as he looked steadfastly toward Heaven, saw it open. And Jesus Himself was standing at the right hand of God, the place He had designated before His crucifixion and resurrection would be His abiding place until the time of the Gentiles should be fulfilled, when He would leave Heaven with a shout of triumph and return to this earth in the clouds of Heaven.

Among the last declarations of Jesus, in which we all find so much comfort in the hour of bereavement, is: "In my

Father's house are many mansions: if it were not so, I would have told you."

When Heaven's music burst upon human ears that first Christmas morning while the shepherds guarded their flocks on the moonlit hills of Judaea, the angels sang: "On earth peace, good will toward men. For unto you is born this day in the city of David a Saviour, which is Christ the Lord."

We have ample proof that Heaven is a real place.

When we've been there ten thousand years,
Bright shining as the sun,
We've no less days to sing God's praise
Than when we first begun.

What A Wonderful Place!

Oh, what a place Heaven is! The Tuileries of the French, the Windsor Castle of the English, the Alhambra of the Spanish, the Schonbrunn of the Austrians, the White House of the United States - these are all dungeons compared with Heaven.

There are mansions there for the redeemed - one for the martyrs with blood-red robes; one for you ransomed from sin; one for me plucked like a brand from the fire.

Look and see - who are climbing the golden stairs, who are walking on the golden streets, who are looking out of the windows? Some whom we knew and loved here on earth. Yes, I know them. My father and mother, blithe and young as they were on their wedding day. Our son and daughter, sweet as they were when they cuddled down to sleep in our arms. My brother and sister, merrier than when we romped and roamed the fields and plucked wild flowers and listened to the whippoorwill as he sang his lonesome song away over in Sleepy Hollow on the old farm in Iowa where we were born and reared.

Cough gone, cancer gone, consumption gone, erysipelas

gone, blindness gone, rheumatism gone, lameness gone, asthma gone, tears gone, groans and sighs gone, sleepless nights gone.

I think it will take some of us a long time to get used to Heaven.

Pastures without one thistle or weed.
Orchestra without one discord.
Violin without a broken string.
Harps all in tune.
The river without a torn or overflowed bank.
The sunrise and sunset swallowed up in the Eternal Day. "For there shall be no night there."

Heaven will be free from all that curses us here.

No sin - no sorrow - no poverty - no sickness - no pain - no want - no aching heads or hearts - no war - no death. No watching the undertaker screw the coffin lid over our loved ones.

When I reach Heaven I won't stop to look for Abraham, Isaac, Jacob, Moses, Joseph, David, Daniel, Peter or Paul. I will rush past them all saying, "Where is Jesus? I want to see Jesus who saved my soul one dark, stormy night in Chicago in 1887."

If we could get a real appreciation of what Heaven is, we would all be so homesick for Heaven the Devil wouldn't have a friend left on earth.

The Bible description of Heaven is: the length and the breadth and height of it are equal. I sat down and took 12 inches for a foot, our standard. That would make it two thousand five hundred miles long, two thousand five hundred miles wide, two thousand five hundred miles high. Made of pure gold like glass. Twelve gates, each gate made of one pearl. The foundations are of precious stones. Imagine eight thousand miles of diamonds, rubies, sapphires, emeralds, topaz, amethysts, jade, garnets!

Someone may say: "Well, that will be pleasant, if true."

Others say: "I hope it's true"; "I wish it were true." IT IS TRUE!

Heaven: Where There Is No More Death

The kiss of reunion at the gate of Heaven is as certain as the goodbye kiss when you drift out with the tide.

> **God holds the key**
> **Of all unknown,**
> **And I am glad.**
> **If other hands should hold the key,**
> **Or if He trusted it to me,**
> **I might be sad.**

Death is a cruel enemy. He robs the mother of her baby, the wife of her husband, the parents of their children, the lover of his intended wife. He robs the nation of its President.

Death is a rude enemy. He upsets our best plans without an apology. He enters the most exclusive circles without an invitation.

Death is an international enemy. There is no nation which he does not visit. The islands of the seas where the black-skinned mothers rock their babies to the lullaby of the ocean's waves. The restless sea. The majestic mountains. All are his haunts.

Death is an untiring enemy. He continues his ghastly work spring, summer, autumn and winter. He never tires in his ceaseless rounds, gathering the spoils of human souls.

But Death is a vanquished enemy. Jesus arose from the dead and abolished Death, although we may be called upon to die.

Death to the Christian is swinging open the door through which he passes into Heaven.

"Aren't you afraid?" said the wife to a dying miner.

"Afraid, lassie? Why should I be? I know Jesus and Jesus knows me."

The house in which we live, "our body," is beginning to lean. The windows rattle. The glass is dim. The shingles are falling off.

> You will reach the river's brink,
> Some sweet day, by and by.
> You will clasp your broken link
> Some sweet day, by and by.

> There's a glorious kingdom waiting
> In the land above the sky.
> Where the saints have been gathering
> Year by year.

> And the days are swiftly passing
> That shall bring the Kingdom nigh.
> For the coming of the Lord
> Draweth near.

Thank God for the rainbow of hope that bends above the graves of our loved ones.

We stand on this side of the grave and mourn as they go. They stand on the other side and rejoice as they come.

> On the Resurrection morning
> Soul and body meet again;
> No more sorrow, no more weeping,
> No more pain.

> Soul and body reunited
> Thenceforth nothing can divide.
> Waking up in Christ's own likeness;
> Satisfied!

On that happy Easter morning,
All the graves their dead restore,
Father, sister, child and mother,
Meet once more.

To that brightest of all meetings
Brings us Jesus Christ, at last,
By the cross through death and judgment,
Holding fast.

The Bible indicates that angels know each other. If they have the power to recognise each other, won't we?

The Bible describes Heaven as a great home circle. It would be a queer home circle if we did not know each other.

The Bible describes death as a sleep. Well, we know each other before we go to sleep, and we know each other when we wake up. Do you imagine we will be bigger fools in Heaven than we are here on earth?

A woman lay dying. She had closed her eyes. Her sister, thinking her dead, commenced the wail of mourning. The dying woman raised her hand and said: "Hush! Hush! I am listening to the breezes waving the branches in the tree of life."

You will be through with your backbiting enemies. They will call you vile names no more. They will no longer misrepresent your good deeds.

Broken hearts will be bound up. Wounds will be healed. Sorrows ended.

The comfort of God is greater than the sorrows of men. I've thanked God a thousand times for the roses but never for the thorns, but now I have leaned to thank Him for the thorns.

You will never be sick again, never be tired again, never weep again.

What's the use of fretting when we are on our way to such a coronation!

Jesus, The Only Way To Heaven

You must know the password if you ever enter Heaven. Jesus said, "I am the way, the truth, and the life; no man cometh unto the Father, but by me."

Here comes a crowd. They cry: "Let me in. I was very useful on earth. I built churches. I endowed colleges. I was famous for my charities. I have done many wonderful things."

"I never knew you."

Another crowd shouts: "We were highly honoured on earth. The world bowed very low before us. now we have come to get our honours in Heaven"

"We never knew you."

Another crowd approaches and says: "We were sinners, wanderers from God. We have come up, not because we deserve Heaven, but because we heard of the saving power of Jesus; and we have accepted Him as our Saviour."

They all cry, "Jesus, Jesus, Thou Son of God, open to us."

They all pass through the pearly gates.

One step this side and you are paupers for eternity. One step on the other side and you are kings and queens for eternity. When I think of Heaven and my entering it, I feel awkward.

Sometimes when I have been exposed to the weather, shoes covered in mud, coat wet and soiled with mud and rain, hair dishevelled, I feel I am not fit to go in and sit among the well-dressed guests.

So I feel that way about Heaven. I need to be washed in the blood of the Lamb and clothed in the robe of Christ's righteousness. I need the pardoning waves of God's mercy to roll over my soul. And, thank God, they have.

If you go first, will you come down halfway and meet me between the willow banks of earth and the palm groves of Heaven? You who have loved ones in Heaven, will you take a pledge with me to meet them when the day dawns and the shadows flee away?

Some who read this are sadly marching into the face of the setting sun. You are sitting by the window of your soul looking out toward the twilight of life's purple glow. You are listening to the music of the breaking waves of life's ebbing tide and longing for the sight of the faces and the sound of voices loved and lost awhile.

But if you have accepted Jesus as your Saviour, at last you will hail the coming morning radiant and glorious when the waves of the sea will become crystal chords in the grand organ of Eternity.

A saint lay dying. She said: "My faith is being tried. The brightness of which you speak I do not have. But I have accepted Jesus as my Saviour; and if God wishes to put me to sleep in the dark, His will be done."

Blessed Hope For The Christian!

Sorrow sometimes plays strange dirges on the heartstrings of life before they break, but the music always has a message of hope.

Should you go first, and I remain
To walk the road alone,
I'll live in memory's garden, dear,
WIth happy days we've known.
In Spring I'll watch for roses red,
When fade the lilacs blue;
In early Fall, when the brown leaves fall,
I'll catch a breath of you.

Should you go first, and I remain
For battles to be fought,
Each thing you've touched along the way
Will be a hallowed spot.
I'll hear your voice, I'll see your smile,
Though blindly I may grope;

The memory of your helping hand
Will buoy me on with hope.

Should you go first, and I remain
To finish with the scroll,
No length'ning shadows shall creep in
To make this life seem droll.
We've known so much of happiness,
We've had our cup of joy;
Ah, memory is one gift of God
That death cannot destroy.

Should you go first, and I remain,
One thing I'd have you do;
Walk slowly down the path of death,
For soon I'll follow you.
I'll want to know each step you take,
That I may walk the same;
For some day - down that lonely road -
You'll hear me call your name.

One day when the children were young. I was romping and playing with them; and I grew tired and lay down to rest. half asleep and half awake I dreamed I journeyed to a far-off land.

It was not Persia, although the Oriental beauty and splendour were there.

It was not India, although the coral strands were there.

It was not Ceylon, although the beauty and spicy perfume of that famous island paradise were there.

It was not Italy, although the dreamy haze of the blue Italian sky beat above me.

It was not California nor Florida, although the soft flower-ladened breezes of the Pacific and the Atlantic were there.

I looked for weeds, briars, thorns, and thistles, but I found none.

I saw the sun in all his meridian glory. I asked, "When will the sun set and grow dark?" They said: "Oh, it never grows dark in this land. There is no night here. Jesus is the light."

I saw the people all clothed in holiday attire with faces wreathed in smiles and halos of glory about their heads. I asked: "When will the working men go by with the calloused hands and empty dinner buckets and faces grimed with dust and toil?" They said; "Oh, we toil not, neither do we sow nor reap in this land."

I strolled out into the suburbs and the hills which would be a fit resting place for the dead to sleep. I looked for monuments, mausoleums, marble slabs, tombs and graves; but saw none. I did see towers, spires and minarets. I asked; "Where do you bury the dead of this great city? Where are the grave diggers? Where are the hearses that haul the dead to their graves?" They said: "Oh, we never die in this land."

I asked: "Where are the hospitals where you take the sick?" Where are the nurses with the panacea and opiates to ease the pain?" They said: "Oh, we are never sick. None ever die in this land."

I asked: "Where do the poor people live? Where are the homes of penury and want?" They said: "Oh, there are no poor in this land. There is no want here. None are ever hungry here."

I was puzzled.

I looked and saw a river. Its waves were breaking against golden and jewel-strewn beaches.

I saw ships with sails of pure silk, bows covered with gold, oars tipped with silver.

I looked and saw a great multitude no man could number, rushing out of jungles of roses, down banks of violets, redolent of eternal Spring, pulsing with bird song and the voices of angels.

I realised Time had ended and Eternity had dawned.

I cried: "Are all here?"

They echoed: "Yes, all here."

And tower and spire and minaret all carolled my welcome

home. And we all went leaping and singing and shouting the eternal praises of God the Father, God the Son, God the Holy Spirit.

Home, home, at last!

Here's to you, my friends,
May you live a hundred years,
Just to help us
Through this vale of tears.

May I live a hundred years
Short just one day,
Because I don't want to be here
After all my friends have gone away.

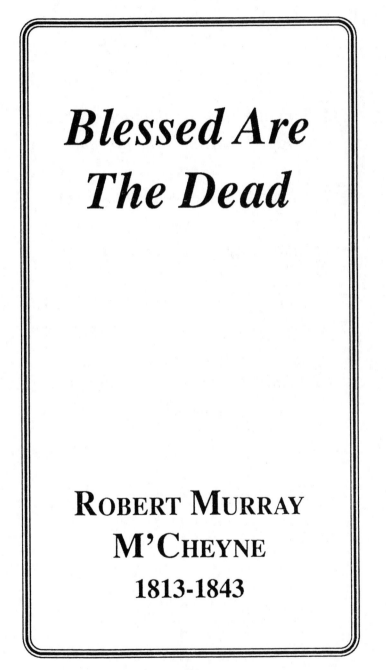

Blessed Are The Dead

ROBERT MURRAY M'CHEYNE

1813-1843

'The light of Heaven is the face of Jesus,
The joy of Heaven is the presence
of Jesus,
The melody of Heaven is the name
of Jesus,
The harmony of Heaven the praise
of Jesus,
The theme of Heaven the work of Jesus,
The employment of Heaven the service
of Jesus,
The fullness of Heaven is Jesus
Himself!'

ANON.

5

Blessed Are The Dead

R. MURRAY M'CHEYNE

"Blessed are the dead which die in the Lord from hence-forth: Yea, saith the Spirit, that they may rest from their labours; and their works do follow them." - Rev. 14:13

There are two remarkable things in the manner in which these words are given to us.

1. They Are The Words Of The Father Echoed Back By The Spirit

"I heard a voice from Heaven." "Yea saith the Spirit." John's eye had been riveted upon the wondrous sight men- tioned in verse 1. A lamb stood on Mount Zion, and one hundred and forty-four thousand redeemed ones following Him whithersoever He goeth, when suddenly a still small voice broke upon his ear, saying, "Write, Blessed are the dead;" and then the Holy Spirit breathed Amen. "Yea, saith the Spirit."

It is written in the law that the testimony of two witnesses is true. Now, here are two witnesses, - the Father of all, and the Holy Spirit the Comforter, both testifying that it is a happy thing to die in the Lord. Is there any of you, God's children, who tremble at the thought of dying? Doth death appear a monster with a dreadful dart, ready to destroy you? Here are two sweet and blessed witnesses who declare that death has lost his sting - that the grave has lost its victory. Listen, and the frown will disappear from the brow of death, - the valley will be filled with light; the Father and the Holy Spirit both unite in saying, "Blessed are the dead."

2. Write

Whatever is written down is more durable, and less liable to be corrupted, than that which is only spoken from mouth to mouth. For this reason, God gave the Israelites the Ten Commandments, written with His own finger on two tables of stone. For the same reason,He commanded them, on the day they passed over Jordan, to set up great stones, and plaster them with plaster, and *write* upon them all the words of that law. For the same reason, God commanded His servants the prophets to *write* their prophecies, and the apostles to *write* their gospels and epistles, so that we have a permanent Bible instead of floating tradition. For this reason *did Job wish* his words to be written. "Oh that my words were written! Oh that they were printed in a book! That they were graven with an iron pen and with lead in the rock for ever! I know that my Redeemer liveth" (Job 19:25). It was one of his precious, ever memorable sayings, - a saying to comfort the heart of a drooping believer in the darkest hour, - *"I know that my Redeemer liveth."* For the same reason did the voice from heaven say, *"Write,"* - do not hear it only, but *write it* - print it in a book - grave it with an iron pen - with lead in the rock for ever.

"Blessed are the dead." Learn the value of this saying. it is a golden saying - there is gold in every syllable of it. it is sweeter than honey and the honeycomb, - more precious than gold, yea, much fine gold. It is precious in the eyes of God. *Write it* deep in your hearts; it will solemnise your life, and will keep you from being led away by its vain show. It will make the syren songs of this world inconvenient and out of tune; it will sweetly sooth you in the hour of adversity; it will rob death of its sting, and the grave of its victory. *Write, write* deep on your heart, "Blessed are the dead which die in the Lord."

Now, consider the *words* themselves.

(1) "Blessed are the dead." - The world say, Blessed are the living; but God says, Blessed are the dead. The world judge of things by sense - as they outwardly appear to men; God judges of things by what they really are in themselves - He looks at things in their real colour and magnitude. The world says, "Better is a living dog than a dead lion." The world look upon some of their families, coming out like a fresh blooming flower in the morning, - their cheeks covered with the bloom of health, their step bounding with elasticity of youth, - riches and luxuries at their command, - long, bright summer days before them. The world says, "There is a happy soul." God takes us into the darkened room, where some child of God lately dwelt. He points to the pale face where death sits enthroned, the cheek wasted by long disease, the eye glazed in death, the stiff hands clasped over the bosom, the friends standing weeping around. and He whispers in our ears, "Blessed are the dead." Ah, dear friends, think a moment! - whether does God or you know best? Who will be found to be in the right at last? Alas, what a vain show you are walking in! Disquieted in vain. "Man that is in honour, and understandeth not, is like the beasts that perish." Even God's children sometimes say, "Blessed are the living." It is a happy thing to live in the favour of God, - to have peace with God, - to frequent the throne of grace, - to burn the perpetual incense of praise, - to meditate on His word, - to hear the preached gospel, - to serve God; even to wrestle, and run, and

fight in His service, is sweet. Still God says, *"Blessed are the dead."* If it be happy to have His smile *here*, how much happier to have it without a cloud *yonder!* If it be sweet to be the growing corn of the Lord *here*, how much better to be gathered into His barn! If it be sweet to have an anchor within the veil, how much better *ourselves* to be *there*, where no gloom can come! In "Thy presence is *fullness* of joy; at Thy right hand are pleasures for evermore." Even *Jesus* felt this, - God attests it. *"Blessed are the dead."*

(2) *Not all the dead*, but those that *"die in the Lord."* It is truly amazing the multitudes that die. "Thou carriest them away as with a flood." Seventy thousand die every day, about fifty every minute, - nearly one every second passing over the verge. Life is like a stream made up of human beings, pouring on, and rushing over the brink into eternity. Are all these blessed? Ah, no. *"Blessed are the dead who die in the Lord."* Of all that vast multitude continually pouring into the eternal world, a little company alone having savingly believed on Jesus. "Strait is the gate and narrow is the way that leadeth unto life and *few* there be that find it." It is not *all* the dead who are blessed. There is no blessing on the Christless dead; they rush into an *undone* eternity, unpardoned, unholy. You may put their body in a splendid coffin; you may print their name in silver on the lid; you may bring the well-attired company of mourners to the funeral, in suits of solemn black; you may lay the coffin slowly in the grave; you may spread the greenest sod above it; you may train the sweetest flowers to grow over it; you may cut a white stone, and grave a gentle epitaph to their memory; - still it is but the funeral of a damned soul. You cannot write *"blessed"* where God has written *"cursed."* "He that believeth shall be saved; he that believeth not shall be damned."

Consider what is implied in the words "in the Lord."

First, *That they were joined to the Lord*. - Union to the Lord has a beginning. Every one that is blessed in dying has been converted. You may dislike the word, but that is the truth.

They were awakening - began to weep - pray - weep as they went to seek the Lord their God. They saw themselves lost, undone, helpless, - that they could not be just with a holy God. They became babes. The Lord Jesus drew near, and revealed Himself. "I am the Bread of Life." "Him that cometh unto Me, I will in nowise cast out." They believed and were happy, - rejoiced in the Lord Jesus, - counted everything but loss of Christ. They gave themselves to the Lord. This was the beginning of their being in Christ.

Dear friends, have you had this beginning? Have you undergone conversion - the new birth - grafting into Christ. Call it by any name you will, have you done the thing: Has this union to Christ taken place in your history? Some say, I do not know. If at any time of your life you had been saved from drowning, - if you were actually drowned and brought to life again, - you would remember it to your dying hour. Much more if you had been brought to Christ. If you had been blind, and by some remarkable operation your eyes were opened when you were full grown, would you ever forget it? So, if you have been truly brought into Christ, you may easily remember it. If not, you will die in your sins. Whither Christ has gone, thither you cannot come. "Except ye repent and be converted, ye shall all likewise perish."

Second, *Perseverance is implied. - Not all* that seem to be branches are branches of the true vine. Many branches fall off the trees when the high winds begin to blow - all that are rotten branches. So in times of temptation, or trial, or persecution, many false professors drop away. Many that seemed to be believers went back, and walked no more with Jesus. They followed Jesus - they prayed with Him - they praised Him; but they went back, and walked no more with him. So is it still. Many among us doubtless seem to be converted; they begin well and promise fair, who will fall off when winter comes. Some have fallen off, I fear, already; some more may be expected to follow. These will not be blessed in dying. Oh, of all death beds, may I be kept from beholding the death bed of the false professor! I have seen it before now, and I trust I may never see it again. They are not blessed after death. The rotten branches will burn more fiercely in the flames. Oh, think what torment it will be, to think that you spent your life in pretending to be a Christian, and lost your opportunity of becoming one indeed! Your hell will be all the deeper, blacker, hotter, that you knew so much of Christ, and were so near Him, and found Him not. Happy are they who endure to the end, who are not moved away from the hope of the gospel, who, when others go away, say, Lord, to whom can we go? In prosperity, they follow the Lord fully; in adversity, they cleave to Him closer still as the trees and strike their roots deeper in storms. Is this your case? - endure it to the end. "Be not moved away from the hope of the gospel" (Col. 1:23). "We are made partakers of Christ, if we hold the beginning of our confidence steadfast unto the end." (Heb. 3:15). Even in the dark valley you will cling to Him still. Come to Him as ye came at first - a guilty creature, clinging to the Lord our Righteousness. Thou wast made sin. This is to die in the Lord, and this is to be blessed.

3. Reasons Why They Are Blessed

(1) *Because of the time* . - "From henceforth." The time of the persecutions of Popery was coming on. He was to wear out the saints of the Most High; he was to overcome and slay the followers of the Lamb. Happy are they that are taken from the evil to come. The righteous perish, and no man layeth it to heart. Merciful men are taken away, none considering that they are taken away from the evil to come. This is one reason why it is better to be with Christ. Persecutions and troubles are not easy to flesh and blood. If in our day we be called to them, we must bear them boldly, knowing that a good reward is provided for those that overcome. See Rev. 2:3: "And hast borne, and hast patience,

and for My name's sake has laboured, and hast not fainted."
But if it will be the will of God to call us away before the day
of trial come, we must say, "Blessed are the dead who die in
the Lord from henceforth." There will be no persecutions
there. All are friends to Jesus there, - every one contending
who shall cast their crowns lowest at His feet, who shall exalt
Him highest in their praise. No discord there. None to rebuke
our song there.

(2) *They rest from their labours* - That which makes
everything laborious here is sin - the opposition of Satan and
the world, and the drag of our old nature. Some believers
have a constant struggle with Satan. He is standing at their
right hand to resist them; he is constantly distracting them in
prayer, hurling fiery darts at their soul, tempting to the most
horrid sin. Their whole life is labour. But when we die in the
Lord, we shall rest from this labour. Satan's work will be
clean done. The accuser of the brethren will no longer annoy.
No lion shall be there, neither shall any ravenous beast go up
thereon, but the redeemed shall walk there. But, above all,
the wicked heart, the old man, the body of sin, makes this life
a dreadful labour. When we wake in the morning it lies like
a weight upon us. When we would run in the way of God's
commandments, it drags us back. When we would fly, it
weighs us down. When we would pray, it fills our mouths
with other things. "O wretched man that I am!" But to depart
and be with Christ, is to be free from this. We shall drop this
body of sin altogether. No more any flesh - all spirit, all new
man; no more weight or drag - we shall rest from our labours.
Oh, it is this makes death in the Lord blessed! We shall not
rest from all work; we shall be as the angels of God - we shall
serve Him day and night in His temple. We shall not rest
from our work, but from our labours. There will be no toil,
no pain, in our work. We shall rest in our work. Oh, let this
make you willing to depart, and make death look pleasant,
and heaven a home. "We shall rest from our labours." It is the
world of holy love, where we shall give free, full, unfettered,

unwearied expression to our love for ever.

(3) *Works follow*. - Our good works done in the name of Jesus shall then be rewarded. *First*, Observe, they shall not go before the soul. It is not on account of them we shall be accepted. We must be accepted *first* altogether on account of *Him* in whom we stand. *Second*, Our evil works shall be forgotten, - buried in the depths of the sea, - forgotten, no more mentioned. *Third*, All that we have done out of love to Jesus shall then be rewarded. We may forget them, and say to Jesus, "When saw we Thee sick, or in prison, and came unto Thee?" But he will not forget them; "Inasmuch as ye have done it unto one of the least of these My brethren, ye have done it unto Me." A cup of cold water shall not go unrewarded.

4. What Followed

The Lord Jesus "put in His sickle and reaped." (See vers. 14,15.)

(1) Learn that the Lord Jesus gathers His sheaves before a storm, just as farmers do; so when you see Him gathering ripe saints, be sure that a storm is near.

(2) Learn that Jesus gathers His saints in love. When Jesus gathers His own, He does it in love. Do not mourn for them as those who have no hope. Jesus has gathered them into His bosom. They shall shine as the sun.

> **When this passing world is done,**
> **When has sunk yon glaring sun,**
> **When we stand with Christ in glory,**
> **Looking o'er life's finished story,**
> **Then, Lord, shall I fully know -**
> **Not till then - how much I owe.**

When I hear the wicked call
On the rocks and hills to fall,
When I see them start and shrink
On the fiery deluge brink,
Then, Lord, shall I fully know -
Not till then - how much I owe.

When I stand before the throne,
Dressed in beauty not my own,
When I see Thee as Thou art,
Love Thee with unsinning heart,
Then, Lord, shall I fully know -
Not till them - how much I owe.

When the praise of heaven I hear,
Loud as thunders to the ear,
Loud as many waters' noise,
Sweet as harp's melodious voice,
Then, Lord, shall I fully know -
Not till then - how much I owe.

Another Five Great Preachers on Heaven . . .

It is certain that all that will go to Heaven hereafter begin their Heaven now, and have their hearts there.

MATTHEW HENRY

When I get to Heaven, I shall see three wonders there – the first wonder will be so see how many people there whom I did not expect to see; the second wonder will be to miss many people whom I did expect to see; and the third and greatest wonder of all will be to find myself there.

JOHN NEWTON

One breath of paradise will extinguish all the adverse winds of earth.

A. W. PINK

Heaven will pay for any loss we may suffer to gain it; but nothing can pay for the loss of Heaven.

RICHARD BAXTER

*If you're not allowed to laugh
in Heaven, I don't want to go there.*

MARTIN LUTHER